Learn Markdown

Practical Guide

A. De Quattro

Copyright © 2024

Practical Guide

1.Introduction to Markdown

In recent years, the Markdown markup language has become one of the most widely used tools for writing and formatting text quickly and easily, thanks to its readability and simplicity. Originally designed as a lightweight markup language, Markdown has found extensive use in contexts ranging from software documentation to article writing, and even for formatting emails and comments on social media. This article provides a comprehensive overview of Markdown, examining its definition, history, and the advantages it offers compared to other markup technologies.

What is Markdown?

Markdown is a markup language created to facilitate writing formatted text using simple and intuitive syntax. Its distinctive feature is that text written in Markdown is easily readable even without being converted into more complex formats like HTML. Unlike heavier markup languages such as HTML, which require extensive and less intuitive tags, Markdown allows text formatting using simple symbols like asterisks, dashes, and hashes, making it accessible to anyone, even without technical expertise.

Markdown enables users to add headings, bullet or numbered lists, hyperlinks, images, code blocks, and much more in a natural and readable way. Markdown's syntax is designed to be non-intrusive, meaning that even without knowledge of the syntax, the text remains comprehensible, avoiding the visual noise caused by tags that characterize languages like HTML or LaTeX.

For example, in Markdown:

- A heading can be created using the `#` symbol, so `# Heading` becomes a level 1 heading.

- Bold text is enclosed by two asterisks `**bold text**`.

- A bullet list is simply a list of lines starting with a dash or asterisk, for example:

```
- Item 1
- Item 2
```

- Hyperlinks are written in this form: `[link text](https://example.com)`.

The simplicity of Markdown makes it especially suitable for writers, developers, and anyone who wants to create structured documents without the complexity of traditional markup languages.

Key Elements of Markdown Syntax

- **Headings**: Using the `#` symbol

followed by a space defines a heading. More `#` symbols indicate a lower-level heading. For example:

```
# Heading 1 creates a level 1 heading.
## Heading 2 creates a level 2 heading.
```

And so on up to level 6.

- **Italic and Bold Text**: Text can be formatted in italics or bold using either one or two asterisks or underscores:

```
*italic* or _italic_
**bold** or __bold__
```

- **Bullet Lists**: Bullet lists can be created using a dash `-`, asterisk `*`, or plus sign `+`. All these symbols work interchangeably:

```
- List item
* List item
+ List item
```

- **Numbered Lists**: Numbered lists are created using numbers followed by a period:

```
1. First item
2. Second item
```

- **Links**: Links can be inserted using this syntax:

   ```
   [link text](URL) like [Google](https://www.google.com)
   ```

- **Images**: The syntax for images is similar to links but with an exclamation mark `!` at the beginning:

   ```
   ![Alt text](image-URL)
   ```

- **Code Blocks**: Code blocks are indicated with three backticks ``` ``` ``` or by indenting the text with four spaces:

```python
print("Hello, world!")
```

History and Origin of Markdown

Markdown was created by John Gruber and Aaron Swartz in 2004 with the goal of providing a markup language that would be readable even in its raw form. The main motivation behind its creation was to simplify writing HTML by making the syntax more understandable and human-readable. The goal was not to replace HTML but rather to create a tool that facilitated structured text writing, which could then be easily converted into HTML or other formats.

John Gruber and Aaron Swartz: The Creators

- **John Gruber**: Gruber, a blogger and

developer, wanted a tool that would make it easier to write content for the web without having to manually write complex HTML tags. His main idea was to create a markup language that was so simple and intuitive that it could be written and read without requiring technical expertise. Before creating Markdown, Gruber had worked on various writing and publishing projects online, and Markdown represented an evolution of these experiences.

- **Aaron Swartz**: Swartz, a computer prodigy and one of the main activists for the free dissemination of online knowledge, collaborated with Gruber in the creation of Markdown. Already known for contributing to the creation of technologies like RSS and Creative Commons, Swartz brought an innovative vision to Markdown, envisioning a future where writing and publishing content could be simple and accessible to everyone.

The first version of Markdown was released in December 2004 and was soon adopted by many blogging platforms, documentation sites, and collaboration services like GitHub and Stack Overflow. Its popularity skyrocketed because it allowed users to create formatted content without worrying about the complexity of HTML or other markup languages.

Evolution and Spread of Markdown

After its initial launch, Markdown saw growing adoption across various contexts. Initially conceived to facilitate blog post writing, its simplicity made it a key tool for many types of projects. The core syntax of Markdown has remained consistent over time, but many extensions have been introduced to meet specific needs in different sectors.

Among the most popular extensions is **Markdown Extra**, which adds advanced features like tables, footnotes, and definition lists. Additionally, numerous Markdown dialects have been developed to tailor it for specific uses, such as **GitHub Flavored Markdown (GFM)**, an extension used primarily in developer collaboration platforms like GitHub. GFM includes features like support for task lists, @mentions, and the ability to add syntax highlighting for code.

Over the years, Markdown's popularity has also driven the development of dedicated editors that make the writing and formatting process even simpler. These editors offer real-time previews, quick conversions to HTML and other formats, and integrations with code versioning systems, making Markdown an essential tool for online collaboration.

Advantages of Using Markdown

Markdown offers numerous advantages that have made it a de facto standard for writing and publishing content online. These advantages manifest in its ease of use, versatility, and ability to adapt to various needs.

1. **Simplicity and Readability**

One of Markdown's main strengths is its simplicity. Unlike other markup languages like HTML or LaTeX, which can be complex and difficult to read in raw form, Markdown was designed to be simple and readable even in its raw format. This means that text written in Markdown can be read and understood by anyone, without needing technical knowledge. Even if the document is never converted to a more complex format like HTML or PDF, it remains readable and comprehensible.

For example, compare a sentence written in HTML and the same sentence written in Markdown:

- HTML: `<strong>Hello</strong>, this is an example of <em>Markdown text</em>!`

- Markdown: `**Hello**, this is an example of *Markdown text*!`

As you can see, the Markdown version is

much clearer and more intuitive than the HTML version, which requires opening and closing tags, cluttering the text's readability.

2. **Versatility and Portability**

Another significant advantage of Markdown is its portability. Markdown is supported by a wide range of platforms, editors, and services, making it an excellent choice for anyone wanting to write content that can easily be converted into different formats, such as HTML, PDF, DOCX, LaTeX, and more.

Markdown is compatible with many popular platforms like GitHub, GitLab, Stack Overflow, Reddit, and many other collaboration tools. This means that once a document is written in Markdown, it can be easily transferred and viewed on various services without complex adaptations.

3. **Ease of Conversion**

Markdown was designed to be easily

convertible into more complex formats. Thanks to the numerous converters available, a Markdown document can be transformed into HTML, PDF, DOCX, and other formats effortlessly. This is especially useful in professional or academic contexts, where documents need to be produced in different formats.

For example, tools like **Pandoc** allow converting Markdown files into a wide range of formats, including:

- HTML for web publishing,

- PDF for printing and offline distribution,

- DOCX for integration with word processing software like Microsoft Word.

4. **Effective Collaboration**

Markdown is widely used in software development projects and online collaboration platforms because it allows multiple users to work together on the same document without worrying about formatting conflicts. Platforms like GitHub use Markdown for README files, comments in pull requests and issues, making it a standard for collaboration among developers.

2.Installation and Configuration of Markdown

Markdown is a simple and intuitive markup language that, despite its lightweight nature, can be integrated and enhanced through a wide variety of editors, plugins, and tools. In this guide, we will explore the installation and configuration of a Markdown environment, focusing on compatible text editors, setting up the environment to work with Markdown, and useful plugins and tools to improve the writing and formatting experience.

Compatible Text Editors

Markdown is supported by a wide range of text editors, from simple editors like Notepad to advanced editors offering live previews, syntax highlighting, and version control integration. Here are some of the most popular options:

1. **Generic Text Editors**

Generic text editors are tools that, while not specifically designed for Markdown, fully support its syntax. They are often chosen for their simplicity and lightweight nature. However, plugins or extensions can be added to enhance Markdown support.

a) Notepad++

Notepad++ is a popular text editor for Windows among programmers and writers. While it doesn't natively offer advanced Markdown features, it can easily be extended with plugins like "MarkdownViewer++," which allows for previewing Markdown text.

Installing Notepad++:

1. Download Notepad++ from the official site (https://notepad-plus-plus.org/).

2. Install the editor following the instructions for your operating system.

3. To add Markdown support, go to

"Plugins" > "Plugins Admin", search for "MarkdownViewer++," and install it.

4. Once installed, you can open an `.md` file and see a live preview.

b) Sublime Text

Sublime Text is a cross-platform text editor (available for Windows, macOS, and Linux) known for its speed and lightweight design. Although it's not optimized for Markdown out of the box, additional packages can be installed to enhance Markdown syntax support.

Installing Sublime Text:

1. Visit the official Sublime Text site (https://www.sublimetext.com/) and download the latest version.

2. Install Sublime Text following the instructions.

3. Install **Package Control** to manage plugins:

- Press `Ctrl + P` to open the console.

   - Type `Install Package Control` and follow the instructions.

4. To enable Markdown support, search for and install the packages "MarkdownEditing" and "Markdown Preview."

c) Visual Studio Code

Visual Studio Code (VS Code) is a free, open-source code editor developed by Microsoft. It is arguably the most popular editor for Markdown due to its powerful features, extensive plugin support, and integration with version control tools like Git.

Installing Visual Studio Code:

1. Download VS Code from the official site (https://code.visualstudio.com/) and install it.

2. To enhance VS Code with advanced Markdown features, open the extension Marketplace and search for "Markdown All in One."

3. Install the "Markdown All in One" extension to improve syntax support, previews, and shortcuts.

2. **Markdown-Specific Editors**

Markdown-specific editors are designed exclusively for Markdown and offer an optimized environment for writing and viewing text. These editors include real-time synchronization between raw text and formatted previews, syntax highlighting, and export tools for various formats like PDF or HTML.

a) Typora

Typora is one of the most popular Markdown editors due to its clean, distraction-free interface. It's a WYSIWYG editor (What You See Is What You Get), meaning there's no separation between raw text and its formatted preview; as you write in Markdown, you immediately see the formatted result.

Installing Typora:

1. Visit the Typora site (https://typora.io/) and download the latest version for your operating system.

2. Follow the installation instructions.

3. Once installed, Typora allows you to write in Markdown with an immediate, direct view of the formatted text.

b) Mark Text

Mark Text is a simple, lightweight, open-source editor specifically designed for Markdown. It offers real-time previews and supports a wide range of extended Markdown features like tables, diagrams, and footnotes.

Installing Mark Text:

1. Visit the official Mark Text repository on GitHub (https://github.com/marktext/marktext) and download the appropriate package for your operating system.

2. Follow the installation instructions for your system.

3. Mark Text is ready to use immediately after installation, with built-in support for a wide range of Markdown extensions.

3. **Online Editors**

Online editors allow users to work on Markdown documents directly in the browser without installing software. These editors are especially useful for distributed teams or for quick access without complex configurations.

a) Dillinger

Dillinger is a free, open-source online Markdown editor that allows you to write, preview, and export Markdown documents in various formats like HTML, PDF, and DOCX. It also supports integration with cloud services like Google Drive, Dropbox, and GitHub.

b) StackEdit

StackEdit is another online Markdown editor offering advanced features like synchronization with Google Drive and Dropbox, real-time preview, and offline mode. It's particularly useful for collaborative writing and cloud file management.

Environment Configuration

To optimize your experience with Markdown, you can configure your working environment to facilitate writing, viewing, and managing Markdown documents. Here are some key configurations that can improve your Markdown experience, regardless of the editor chosen.

1. **Add Live Preview Support**

One of the best ways to enhance the Markdown writing experience is to enable live preview, allowing you to immediately see how formatted text will look without exporting or converting the document each time.

- In editors like **VS Code**, you can enable the preview with the command `Ctrl + Shift + V` (or `Cmd + Shift + V` on macOS).

- In **Sublime Text**, installing plugins like "Markdown Preview" provides the option to open a preview in a separate window or directly within the editor.

2. **Enable Syntax Highlighting**

Syntax highlighting improves the readability of Markdown text, making it easy to distinguish between normal text, headers, links, and code. Most modern editors support syntax highlighting for Markdown, but in some cases, specific plugins or packages may need to be installed.

- **VS Code** natively supports syntax highlighting for Markdown, but you can enhance its appearance with extensions like "Markdown Enhanced."

- **Sublime Text** requires the installation of packages like "MarkdownEditing" to improve syntax highlighting.

3. **Integrate Export Tools**

Markdown is often used as a starting point for creating documents in other formats like HTML, PDF, or DOCX. To streamline this process, many editors offer built-in export tools or plugins that automate conversion.

- In **VS Code**, you can install the "Markdown PDF" extension to quickly export Markdown documents to PDF.

- In **Typora**, export support is already built-in, allowing you to export your documents to PDF, Word, LaTeX, and other formats with just a few clicks.

4. **Integration with Git and Version Control**

If you're using Markdown for project documentation or collaborative writing, it's advisable to integrate your environment with a version control system like **Git**. This allows you to manage document changes, track revisions, and easily collaborate with other team members.

- **VS Code** offers native Git and GitHub integration, making it easy to manage version control directly from the editor.

- In **Sublime Text**, plugins like "GitGutter" can be used to view real-time changes and manage Git repositories.

Useful Plugins and Tools

Beyond the basic editors and configurations, there are numerous plugins and tools that can further enrich your Markdown experience, making writing more efficient and productive. Here are some of the most useful plugins and tools:

1. **Markdown Lint**

Markdown Lint is a tool that helps maintain a consistent writing style and error-free formatting. It scans Markdown files for issues like missing headers, overly long lines, or incorrectly indented lists. It's available as a plugin for various editors, including VS Code and Sublime Text.

2. **Markdown Table Generator**

Creating tables in Markdown can be cumbersome since you need to manually align the `|` characters that separate columns. A helpful tool for simplifying table creation is the **Markdown Table Generator**, available as a plugin or an online tool that generates ready-to-use tables that can be pasted directly into your Markdown document.

3. **PlantUML for Diagrams**

If you need to include diagrams or charts in your Markdown documents, tools like **PlantUML** can be used. PlantUML allows you to create UML diagrams directly within your Markdown files using simple text syntax. This tool is especially useful for documenting complex software and systems.

4. **Pandoc**

Pandoc is a powerful open-source document converter that allows you to transform Markdown files into a wide range of formats, including HTML, LaTeX, PDF, and DOCX. Pandoc is an essential tool for those who frequently convert Markdown documents into other formats for publishing or distribution.

Installing Pandoc:

1. Visit the official Pandoc site (https://pandoc.org/) and download the appropriate version for your operating system.

2. Install Pandoc following the instructions.

3. Once installed, you can convert your Markdown files using the terminal, for example:

   ```bash
   ```

```
pandoc document.md -o document.pdf
```

5. **Mermaid for Flowcharts**

Mermaid is another useful extension for creating diagrams and charts in Markdown. Mermaid supports generating flowcharts, Gantt charts, and other types of visualizations. It can be used in editors like VS Code and GitHub to enhance documentation with dynamically generated visuals.

Markdown is a versatile and widely used

markup language, and with the right environment configuration and tools, it becomes a powerful tool for writers, developers, and technical communicators. Whether you're using a generic text editor, a Markdown-specific editor, or an online editor, there's a wide variety of plugins and tools available to enhance your writing experience, from syntax highlighting and live previews to version control integration and document export.

3. Basic Elements of Markdown

Markdown is a lightweight markup language that allows you to format text in a simple and efficient way, while keeping the content readable even in raw format. This guide will cover the fundamental elements of Markdown in detail, including text syntax, creating lists, inserting links, and images. Practical examples will help you understand how to use these tools to create well-formatted documents quickly and intuitively.

Text Syntax

One of the main aspects of Markdown is text formatting. Markdown allows you to create **bold text**, *italic text*, and more with simple and easy-to-remember syntax.

Bold and Italic

Markdown makes it easy to apply bold and italic styles to text without needing to use complex HTML tags. The syntax is minimalistic and straightforward.

- **Bold**: Bold text is created by enclosing the word or phrase in two asterisks `**` or two underscores `__`.

Example of bold text:

```markdown
**This is bold text**
```

Result:

This is bold text

- *Italic*: To apply italics, simply enclose the

word or phrase in a single asterisk `*` or a single underscore `_`.

Example of italic text:

```markdown
*This is italic text*
```

Result:

This is italic text

- **Bold and Italic**: You can combine both styles by using three asterisks `***` or three underscores `___` to apply both bold and italic.

Example of bold and italic:

```markdown
***This text is bold and italic***
```

Result:

This text is bold and italic

Underlined and Strikethrough

Although underline is not directly supported in standard Markdown, you can simulate it using inline HTML. On the other hand, strikethrough text is directly supported by extended Markdown syntax.

- **Underline**: To underline text, you can use the HTML `<u>` tag.

Example of underlined text:

```markdown
<u>This text is underlined</u>
```

Result:

<u>This text is underlined</u>

- ~~**Strikethrough**~~: Strikethrough text is achieved by enclosing the word or phrase in two tildes `~~`.

Example of strikethrough:

```markdown
~~This text is strikethrough~~
```

Result:

~~This text is strikethrough~~

Lists

Lists are a common way to organize information in a structured and readable manner. Markdown offers various types of lists, including bullet points, numbered lists, and definition lists.

Bullet Points

Bullet points are useful for listing items without a specific order. You can use the hyphen `-`, asterisk `*`, or the plus symbol `+` to create a bullet point.

Example of a bullet point list:

```markdown
- First item
- Second item
  - Sub-item 1
  - Sub-item 2
* Third item
+ Fourth item
```

Result:

- First item
- Second item
  - Sub-item 1
  - Sub-item 2
* Third item

+ Fourth item

As you can see, you can also nest lists by simply adding two spaces before the symbol of the sub-item.

Numbered Lists

Numbered lists are used to show an ordered sequence of items. In Markdown, you can create numbered lists by simply writing the number followed by a period.

Example of a numbered list:

```markdown
1. First step
2. Second step
3. Third step
   1. Sub-step 1
```

2. Sub-step 2
```

**Result**:

1. First step
2. Second step
3. Third step
   1. Sub-step 1
   2. Sub-step 2

Numbered lists can also have nested sub-items using the same indentation (spaces).

#### Definition Lists

Definition lists are not supported in standard Markdown, but some Markdown dialects, like **Markdown Extra**, include them. They are
```

useful for defining terms with descriptions.

Example of a definition list:

```markdown
Term
: Description of the term

Another term
: Another description
```

Result:

Term
: Description of the term

Another term

: Another description

This syntax is particularly useful for creating glossaries or documents where terms need detailed explanations.

Links

Markdown allows you to insert both internal (within the same document) and external links (to other web pages). You can also create anchor links to specific sections of a page.

Internal and External Links

Links in Markdown are defined using the following syntax:

```markdown
[Link text](URL)
```

```

Example of an external link:

```markdown

[Visit the official Markdown site](https://www.markdownguide.org)

```

Result:

[Visit the official Markdown site](https://www.markdownguide.org)

Internal Links

Internal links point to another section within the same document. To create an internal link, you must first define an anchor using headings. In Markdown, headings are
```

automatically anchored by using their text in lowercase and separating words with dashes.

Example:

```markdown
## Example Section

Go to the [Example Section](#example-section)
```

Result:

Go to the [Example Section](#example-section)

Anchor Links

If you want to link to a specific part of an external or internal page, you can use an anchor. Anchors work in combination with HTML IDs or with titles automatically converted to anchors.

Example of an anchor link:

```markdown
[Visit the installation section](https://example.com#installation)
```

Result:

[Visit the installation section](https://example.com#installation)

Anchors are very useful for technical documentation or long web pages where you need to refer to specific sections.

Images

Markdown provides a simple way to embed images within text. The syntax is very similar to that of links, but it includes an exclamation mark `!` at the beginning.

Inserting Images

To insert an image, use the following syntax:

```markdown
![Alt text](Image_URL)
```

- **Alt text**: Describes the image and is shown if the image does not load.

- **Image URL**: The path to the image (can be an online URL or a local path).

Example:

```markdown
![Markdown Logo](https://markdown-here.com/img/icon256.png)
```

Result:

![Markdown Logo](https://markdown-here.com/img/icon256.png)

Linked Images

You can also make an image clickable, turning it into a link. The syntax is a combination of the link and image syntax.

Example of a linked image:

```markdown

[![Markdown Logo](https://markdown-here.com/img/icon256.png)](https://www.markdownguide.org)

```

Result:

[![Markdown Logo](https://markdown-here.com/img/icon256.png)](https://www.markdownguide.org)

In this case, the image becomes a clickable link that leads to the specified URL.

By using these techniques, you can create structured, well-formatted, and easily readable documents. Markdown is an essential tool for anyone working with text, documentation, or web content.

4. Advanced Markdown Formatting

Markdown is known for its simple and lightweight syntax, but it also supports numerous advanced formatting tools that allow you to create complex, structured documents. In this guide, we'll explore the advanced features of Markdown, with a focus on blockquotes, code, and tables. These elements are essential for enhancing the readability and clarity of technical documents, blog posts, and other content formats.

Blockquotes

Blockquotes in Markdown are used to highlight text blocks or include external references. They are a simple way to draw attention to important sections or include quotes from other sources. The syntax for blockquotes is straightforward and clean.

How to Create a Blockquote

Blockquotes are created by using the `>` symbol at the beginning of a line. If you want to include multiple lines of text, each line must start with `>`.

Single blockquote example:

```markdown
> This is an example of a blockquote.
```

Result:

> This is an example of a blockquote.

Multiple and Nested Blockquotes

You can create multiple levels of blockquotes

by nesting more `>` symbols.

Example of nested blockquotes:

```markdown
> This is the first level of blockquote.
>
> > This is the second level of blockquote.
>
> > > This is the third level of blockquote.
```

Result:

> This is the first level of blockquote.
>
> > This is the second level of blockquote.
>

> > > This is the third level of blockquote.

Nested blockquotes are useful for including secondary quotes or emphasizing different content layers.

Blockquotes with Other Elements

Markdown also allows you to combine blockquotes with other formatting elements, such as lists and links.

Blockquote with list example:

```markdown
> This is an example of a blockquote with a list:
> - First item
> - Second item
```

Result:

> This is an example of a blockquote with a list:

> - First item

> - Second item

Blockquote with link example:

```markdown
> "Simplicity is the ultimate sophistication." - [Leonardo da Vinci](https://en.wikipedia.org/wiki/Leonardo_da_Vinci)
```

Result:

> "Simplicity is the ultimate sophistication." - [Leonardo da Vinci](https://en.wikipedia.org/wiki/Leonardo_da_Vinci)

Code

Markdown supports various ways to format code, making it an excellent choice for technical documentation and writing programming-related posts. You can insert inline code (within a sentence) or create separate formatted code blocks.

Inline Code

Inline code is used to highlight small code snippets within a line of text. You do this using single backticks `` ` ``.

Inline code example:

```markdown

To display the contents of a directory, use the `ls` command.

```

Result:

To display the contents of a directory, use the `ls` command.

This type of formatting is useful when you want to include brief references to commands or variables within the flow of your text without breaking it up.

Code Blocks

To format code blocks in Markdown, you can use several techniques. The most common is to enclose the code between three consecutive backticks ``` ``` or indent each line with four spaces. Code blocks also support syntax highlighting, improving readability when writing programming documents.

Code Block without Syntax Highlighting

Here is an example of a code block without syntax highlighting:

```markdown
```

def greet():

   print("Hello, world!")

```

```

Result:

```
def greet():
    print("Hello, world!")
```

Code Block with Syntax Highlighting

Markdown supports syntax highlighting for various programming languages, making the code more readable. To specify the language for the code block, add the name of the language right after the opening three backticks.

Example with syntax highlighting for Python:

````markdown
```python
def greet():
```
````

    print("Hello, world!")
```

```

Result:

```python
def greet():
    print("Hello, world!")
```

Markdown will automatically recognize the language and apply the corresponding highlighting. You can use this approach for any supported language, such as JavaScript, HTML, CSS, and many more.

Indented Code Blocks

Another way to create code blocks is by indenting each line with four spaces or a tab. This technique doesn't allow syntax highlighting, but it's useful when working with Markdown in environments that don't support multiple backticks.

Example:

```markdown

    def greet():

        print("Hello, world!")
```


Result:

    def greet():

        print("Hello, world!")

Tables

Tables in Markdown are a powerful tool for organizing data in a readable, structured format. While creating tables in Markdown requires attention to formatting, once you grasp the basics, you can use them effectively.

Creating Tables

To create a table in Markdown, use the `|` characters to separate columns and dashes `-` to create the header row. Spaces inside the cells are optional but make the table more readable.

Example of a simple table:

```markdown
| Column 1 | Column 2 | Column 3 |
| -------- | -------- | -------- |
| Data 1   | Data 2   | Data 3   |
```

| Data 4 | Data 5 | Data 6 |
```

**Result**:

| Column 1 | Column 2 | Column 3 |
| -------- | -------- | -------- |
| Data 1  | Data 2  | Data 3  |
| Data 4  | Data 5  | Data 6  |

#### Table Formatting

Markdown provides some basic options for table formatting, such as column alignment. You can specify text alignment within each column by using colons `:` in the header separator row.

##### Left Alignment
```

To align text to the left, add a `:` on the left side of the dashes.

Example:

```markdown
| Column 1 | Column 2 | Column 3 |
|:-------- | -------- | -------- |
| Left     | Center   | Right    |
| Left     | Center   | Right    |
```

Result:

Column 1	Column 2	Column 3
Left	Center	Right

| Left | Center | Right |

Right Alignment

To align text to the right, add a `:` on the right side of the dashes.

Example:

```markdown
| Column 1 | Column 2 | Column 3 |
| -------- | --------:| --------:|
| Left     | Center   | Right    |
| Left     | Center   | Right    |
```

Result:

Column 1	Column 2	Column 3
Left	Center	Right
Left	Center	Right

Center Alignment

To center-align text, add colons `:` on both sides of the dashes.

Example:

```markdown
| Column 1 | Column 2 | Column 3 |
|:--------:|:--------:| --------:|
| Left     | Center   | Right    |
| Left     | Center   | Right    |
```

Result:

Column 1	Column 2	Column 3
Left	Center	Right
Left	Center	Right

Tables with Long Rows and Multiple Columns

When working with tables that contain many rows or columns, it's important to maintain the readability of the Markdown file. You can use multiple lines of text inside cells and manage columns of different widths while keeping a clean structure.

Example:

```markdown
| Product      | Price   | Description
|
| -------------- | ------- |
---------------------------------------- |
| Laptop       | €1000   | A powerful laptop for work         |
| Smartphone   | €600    | A versatile and portable device    |
| Tablet       | €400    | Perfect for content consumption    |
```

Result:

| Product | Price | Description
|
| -------------- | ------- |
-- |
| Laptop | €1000 | A powerful laptop for work |

| Smartphone | €600 | A versatile and portable device |
| Tablet | €400 | Perfect for content consumption |

Combining Tables with Other Formatting Elements

You can also combine tables with other Markdown features, such as bold, italic, or even links within table cells.

Example:

```markdown
| Product       | Price    | Description |
| ------------- | -------  | --------------------------------------- |
| **Laptop**    | *€1000*  | [Click here](https://example.com) for more information |
```

| Smartphone | €600 | A versatile and portable device |
| Tablet | €400 | Perfect for content consumption |

```

**Result**:

| Product | Price | Description |
| -------------- | ------- | ---------------------------------------- |
| **Laptop** | *€1000* | [Click here](https://example.com) for more information |
| Smartphone | €600 | A versatile and portable device |
| Tablet | €400 | Perfect for content consumption |

Markdown offers a variety of advanced tools to format text and present information clearly
```

and effectively. Blockquotes are a great way to highlight important content, while its support for code makes it ideal for technical documentation. Although tables may seem complex initially, they provide a structured solution for organizing data. With practice, advanced Markdown usage becomes natural and helps improve the quality and readability of your documents.

5. Content Structures in Markdown

Markdown is a lightweight markup language designed to simplify the writing of formatted text without complications. Let's explore the advanced content structures of Markdown and how they can be applied in different contexts, such as online publishing, static website generation, and collaboration in software projects. This comprehensive guide will cover headings, horizontal lines, footnotes, Markdown extensions, and how to use Markdown for the web and in collaboration.

Headings

Headings are one of the fundamental elements of Markdown, used to organize and structure content into clear, hierarchical sections. Markdown offers six levels of headings, which correspond to HTML tags `<h1>` to `<h6>`. Each heading level represents a different degree of importance or section.

Heading Levels

The syntax for headings is very simple. Just use the `#` symbol followed by a space. The number of `#` symbols determines the heading level.

- **First-level heading (`<h1>`)**: Used for main titles.

Example:

```markdown
# This is a first-level heading
```

Result:

This is a first-level heading

- **Second-level heading (`<h2>`)**: Used for subtitles or main sections.

    Example:

    ```markdown
    ## This is a second-level heading
    ```

    Result:

    ## This is a second-level heading

- **Third-level heading (`<h3>`)**: Used for subsections.

    Example:

```markdown
### This is a third-level heading
```

Result:

This is a third-level heading

- **Fourth-level heading (`<h4>`)**: Used for further subdivisions.

Example:

```markdown
#### This is a fourth-level heading
```

Result:

This is a fourth-level heading

- **Fifth-level heading (`<h5>`)**: Used for more detailed subdivisions.

Example:

```markdown
##### This is a fifth-level heading
```

Result:

This is a fifth-level heading

- **Sixth-level heading (`<h6>`)**: Used for minor subdivisions.

Example:

```markdown
###### This is a sixth-level heading
```

Result:

This is a sixth-level heading

Headings not only enhance readability but also facilitate navigation in long documents, especially when using tools that automatically generate tables of contents based on headings.

Horizontal Lines

Horizontal lines are used to separate sections of content within a document. In Markdown, horizontal lines can be created using three or more hyphens `---`, asterisks `***`, or underscores `___`. These elements produce a continuous horizontal line, helping to visually separate sections.

Creating a Horizontal Line

Example of a horizontal line with hyphens:

```markdown
---
```

Result:

Example of a horizontal line with asterisks:

```markdown
***
```

Result:

***

Example of a horizontal line with underscores:

```markdown
___
```

Result:

___

Horizontal lines are particularly useful when you want to visually separate different sections of content or create a visual pause in the document.

Footnotes

Footnotes are a useful way to provide additional information or citations without interrupting the flow of the text. Standard Markdown does not directly support footnotes, but some Markdown extensions and dialects, such as **Markdown Extra** or **GitHub Flavored Markdown**, do.

Footnote Syntax

In Markdown Extra, footnotes are created using a specific syntax. Here's how it's done:

1. **Insert a footnote**: Use the symbol `[^]` followed by the footnote name.

Example:

```markdown
This is a text with a footnote[^1].
```

2. **Define the footnote content**: At the end of the document or section, define the footnote with the same name used.

Example:

```markdown
[^1]: This is the content of the footnote.
```

Result:

This is a text with a footnote[^1].

[^1]: This is the content of the footnote.

Footnotes are useful for including detailed explanations, citations, or additional information without cluttering the main body of the text.

Markdown Extensions

Markdown, in its basic form, offers a limited syntax. However, there are numerous extensions and Markdown variants that introduce additional features, enhancing formatting and content management. Some of the most popular extensions include:

Markdown Extra

Markdown Extra extends Markdown syntax with new features, such as footnotes, tables, and advanced list and heading syntax.

- **Tables**: Markdown Extra supports tables with a syntax similar to the one shown above.

- **Footnotes**: As described above, Markdown Extra supports footnotes.

Table example with Markdown Extra:

```markdown
| Name  | Age |
| ----- | --- |
| Alice | 30  |
| Bob   | 25  |
```

Result:

Name	Age
Alice	30
Bob	25

GitHub Flavored Markdown (GFM)

GitHub Flavored Markdown is a variant of Markdown used on GitHub. It includes platform-specific extensions, such as:

- **Tables**: Similar to those in Markdown Extra.
- **Task lists**: Checklists that allow you to mark items as complete.

Task list example in GFM:

```markdown
- [x] Completed
- [ ] Not completed
```

Result:

- [x] Completed
- [ ] Not completed

Pandoc

Pandoc is a document conversion tool that supports a wide range of Markdown formats, including advanced and custom versions.

- **Support for different syntaxes**: Pandoc allows you to use various Markdown dialects and convert documents between different formats.

Pandoc usage example:

```markdown
# Title

- List
```

Pandoc can convert this to HTML, PDF, and many other formats.

Markdown for the Web

Markdown is often used to create web content and online documentation. Its features make it ideal for publishing on online platforms, generating static websites, and integrating into content management systems (CMS).

Publishing on Online Platforms

Markdown is supported by many online platforms, such as blogs, forums, and documentation sites. Using Markdown on these platforms offers numerous benefits:

- **Ease of use**: Writing in Markdown is faster and more intuitive than using HTML editors or WYSIWYG tools.

- **Portability**: Markdown documents can be easily converted into HTML and published online.

Blog post example:

```markdown
# Welcome to My Blog

This is my first post! **Hope you enjoy it**.
```

- Point 1

- Point 2

```


**Result**:

# Welcome to My Blog

This is my first post! **Hope you enjoy it**.

- Point 1

- Point 2

#### Generating Static Websites

Markdown is commonly used in generating static websites, thanks to tools like **Jekyll**, **Hugo**, and **MkDocs**.
```

These tools allow you to automatically generate websites from Markdown files, providing a lightweight and scalable solution for publishing content.

- **Jekyll**: Used with GitHub Pages to create static websites directly from Markdown files.

  Example of a Jekyll site structure:

  ```
  _posts/
    2024-01-01-post.md
  _config.yml
  index.md
  ```

- **Hugo**: A static site generator that uses Markdown to create content.

Hugo command to generate the site:

```bash
hugo new posts/my-first-post.md
```

- **MkDocs**: A tool for creating technical documentation using Markdown.

MkDocs configuration example:

```yaml
site_name: My Docs
nav:
  - Home: index.md
  - About: about.md
```

Use in Content Management Systems (CMS)

Many modern CMSs support Markdown for content management, allowing users to write and format content using lightweight syntax without the need for complex editors.

- **WordPress**: Some plugins allow the use of Markdown for posts and pages.
- **Ghost**: A blogging platform that supports Markdown for writing posts and pages.

Ghost post example:

```markdown
# Post Title
```

This is a paragraph with **bold** and *italic* text.

```

### Markdown and Collaboration

Markdown is widely used in collaborative environments, especially in software development. Its simple formatting capabilities and compatibility with version control systems make it a valuable tool for documentation and project management.

#### Version Control with Git

Git is a version control system commonly used with Markdown to manage documents and source code. Markdown is often used to write documentation, README files, and changelogs in Git projects.
```

- **README.md**: A README file written in Markdown that provides information about the project.

README.md example:

```markdown
# Project Name

This is a sample project.

## Installation

```bash
git clone https://github.com/sample/project.git
cd project
```

Contributors
```

- Alice

- Bob
```

- **Changelog.md**: A file that lists the changes and versions of the project.

Changelog example:

```markdown
# Changelog

## [1.0.0] - 2024-01-01

- First version released.
```
```

Documentation in Software Projects

Markdown is often used to write documentation in software projects because of its readability and ease of use. Markdown documents can include developer guides, API documentation, and usage instructions.

- **API Documentation**: Use Markdown to document APIs and their features.

API documentation example:

```markdown
# Sample API

## GET /api/user

Gets user details.
```

Response

```json
{
 "id": 1,
 "name": "Alice"
}
```

```

- **Usage Guides**: Write usage guides for software products using Markdown.

Usage guide example:

```markdown

# Installation Guide

1. Clone the repository.
2. Install dependencies.
3. Run the application.

```

Markdown's versatility and widespread use make it an essential tool for content creation, publishing, and collaboration.
```

6. Markdown Glossary

To fully understand the use and features of Markdown, it's helpful to know some key terms and concepts. This glossary provides a detailed overview of the main terms and elements associated with Markdown.

1. **Markdown**

Definition: Markdown is a lightweight markup language designed to facilitate the writing of formatted documents in plain text. It was created by John Gruber in 2004 with the aim of making formatted document writing simpler and more readable.

Example: Using Markdown, you can write:

```markdown
```

First-Level Heading

This is a paragraph with **bold** and *italic* text.

```

**Result**:

# First-Level Heading

This is a paragraph with **bold** and *italic* text.

### 2. **Syntax**

**Definition**: The syntax of Markdown is the set of rules that determines how text should be formatted. The syntax is designed to be simple and readable, even in plain text.

**Example**: To create a bullet list, use the `-` or `*` character:
```

```markdown
- Item 1
- Item 2
```

Result:

- Item 1
- Item 2

3. **Headings**

Definition: Headings in Markdown are used to define the titles and subtitles of a document. There are six levels of headings, marked by the number of `#`.

Example:

```markdown
# First-Level Heading

## Second-Level Heading

### Third-Level Heading
```

Result:

First-Level Heading

Second-Level Heading

Third-Level Heading

4. **Bold**

Definition: Bold is a text style that emphasizes content, making it visually more prominent. In Markdown, bold text is created using double asterisks `**` or double underscores `__`.

Example:

```markdown
**Bold Text**
__Bold Text__
```

Result:

Bold Text

__Bold Text__

5. **Italic**

Definition: Italic is a text style that slants the content to emphasize or differentiate text. In Markdown, italic text is created using a single asterisk `*` or a single underscore `_`.

Example:

```markdown
*Italic Text*
_Italic Text_
```

Result:

Italic Text

Italic Text

6. **Horizontal Lines**

Definition: Horizontal lines are used to visually separate sections of a document. In Markdown, you can create them with three or more hyphens `---`, asterisks `***`, or underscores `___`.

Example:

```markdown
---

***

___
```

Result:

***

___

7. **Bullet Lists**

Definition: Bullet lists are used to create an unordered list of items. In Markdown, bullet lists are created using `-`, `*`, or `+`.

Example:

```markdown
- Item 1
- Item 2
  - Subitem 1
  - Subitem 2
```

Result:

- Item 1

- Item 2

  - Subitem 1

  - Subitem 2

8. **Numbered Lists**

Definition: Numbered lists are used to create an ordered list of items. In Markdown, numbered lists are created using numbers followed by a period `.`.

Example:

```markdown
1. First item
2. Second item
   1. Subitem 1
   2. Subitem 2
```

Result:

1. First item
2. Second item
    1. Subitem 1
    2. Subitem 2

9. **Links**

Definition: Links in Markdown allow you to insert hyperlinks to web pages or other resources. You can include both internal and external links.

Example:

- **External Link**:

```markdown
[Google](https://www.google.com)
```

Result:

[Google](https://www.google.com)

- **Internal Link**:

```markdown
[Internal Section](#internal-section)
```

Result:

[Internal Section](#internal-section)

10. **Images**

Definition: In Markdown, images can be inserted using a syntax similar to links but preceded by an exclamation mark `!`.

Example:

```markdown
![Alt text](https://www.example.com/image.jpg "Image Title")
```

Result:

![Alt text](https://www.example.com/image.jpg "Image Title")

11. **Inline Code**

Definition: Inline code is used to include small snippets of code within text. In Markdown, inline code is enclosed in two backticks `` ` ` ``.

Example:

```markdown
To use the `print()` function, just call it in your script.
```

Result:

To use the `print()` function, just call it in your script.

12. **Code Blocks**

Definition: Code blocks are used to format and display larger blocks of code. In Markdown, code blocks can be created using three backticks ``` ``` ```, followed by the programming language (optional) for syntax highlighting.

Example:

```markdown
```python
def hello_world():
    print("Hello, world!")
```
```

Result:

```python
```

    def hello_world():
        print("Hello, world!")
```

### 13. **Tables**

**Definition**: Tables in Markdown are used to organize data into rows and columns. The table syntax is relatively simple and can include headers and data cells.

**Example**:

```markdown
| Name    | Age | City   |
|---------|-----|--------|
| Alice   | 30  | Rome   |
| Bob     | 25  | Milan  |
| Charlie | 35  | Naples |

```

Result:

Name	Age	City
Alice	30	Rome
Bob	25	Milan
Charlie	35	Naples

14. **Blockquotes**

Definition: Blockquotes are used to highlight or quote text. In Markdown, blockquotes are created using the `>` symbol.

Example:

```markdown

> This is a blockquote in Markdown.
```

Result:

> This is a blockquote in Markdown.

15. **Footnotes**

Definition: Footnotes allow you to add annotations or references without interrupting the main flow of the text. They are not supported by standard Markdown syntax but are available in extensions like Markdown Extra and GitHub Flavored Markdown.

Example (Markdown Extra):

```markdown
This is a text with a footnote[^1].

[^1]: This is the content of the footnote.
```

Result:

This is a text with a footnote[^1].

[^1]: This is the content of the footnote.

16. **Horizontal Lines**

Definition: Horizontal lines are used to visually separate sections of the document. They can be created using three or more hyphens, asterisks, or underscores.

Example:
```

```markdown

---

***

___
```

Result:

***

___

17. **Markdown Extensions**

Definition: Markdown extensions are additions to the basic syntax to provide extra features. Some popular extensions include

Markdown Extra, GitHub Flavored Markdown (GFM), and Pandoc.

Example of Markdown Extra:

- **Footnotes**:

  ```markdown
  This is a text with a footnote[^1].

  [^1]: Footnote details.
  ```

Example of GitHub Flavored Markdown (GFM):

- **Tables**:

  ```markdown
  ```

Column 1	Column 2
Value 1	Value 2
Value 3	Value 4
```

### 18. **Markdown for the Web**

**Definition**: Markdown is widely used for creating web content due to its readability and ease of use. Markdown files can be converted into HTML for publishing on websites.

**Example**:

```markdown
# Welcome to my site

This is a welcome paragraph.

![Logo](https://www.example.com/logo.png)

```

Result:

Welcome to my site

This is a welcome paragraph.

![Logo](https://www.example.com/logo.png)

19. **Static Website Generation**

Definition: Static website generators use Markdown to create content and generate websites. Tools like Jekyll, Hugo, and MkDocs are popular for this purpose.
```

Example of Jekyll:

- **Jekyll Site Structure**:

  ```plaintext
  _posts/
    2024-01-01-post.md
  _config.yml
  index.md
  ```

Example of Hugo:

- **Command to Create a New Post**:

  ```bash
  hugo new posts/my-first-post.md
  ```

20. **Use in CMS**

Definition: Content Management Systems (CMS) often support Markdown for creating and managing content. This allows users to use simple syntax to format text within the CMS.

Example in WordPress (using a plugin):

```markdown
# Post Title

This is a text with **bold** and *italic* formatting.
```

Example in Ghost:

```markdown
# Post Title

This is a paragraph with **bold** and *italic* text.
```

21. **Version Control with Git**

Definition: Git is a distributed version control system used to manage and version Markdown documents, including README files, changelogs, and project documentation.

Example README.md:

```markdown
```

Project Name

This project is a Markdown demo.

Installation

```bash
git clone https://github.com/user/project.git
cd project
npm install
```

```

### 22. **Documentation in Software Projects**

**Definition**: Markdown is used to write technical documentation in software projects, including developer guides, API
```

documentation, and release notes.

Example API Documentation:

```markdown
# Example API

## GET /api/user

### Parameters

- `id`: User ID.

### Response

```json
{
  "name": "Alice",

```
  "email": "alice@example.com"
}
```

```

With this glossary, you should have a comprehensive understanding of the main terms and concepts associated with Markdown. Markdown is a powerful tool for creating documents and web content in a simple and readable way, and knowing these terms will help you make the most of its capabilities.
```

Index

1. Introduction to Markdown pg.4

2. Installation and Configuration of Markdown pg.18

3. Basic Elements of Markdown pg.33

4. Formattazione avanzata di Markdown pg.51

5. Content Structures in Markdown pg.72

6. Markdown Glossary pg.98